(some of)

The Adventures of Carlyle,

My Imaginary Friend

Winner of the Iowa Poetry Prize

(some of)

The Adventures of Carlyle,

My Imaginary Friend

BY DAINIS HAZNERS

University

of Iowa Press

Iowa City

University of Iowa Press, Iowa City 52242

Copyright © 2004 by Dainis Hazners

Printed in the United States of America

Design by Richard Hendel

http://www.uiowa.edu/uiowapress

Printed on acid-free paper

Library of Congress Cataloging-in-Publication Data
Hazners, Dainis, 1957–.
(Some of) the adventures of Carlyle, my imaginary friend / by Dainis Hazners.
p.   cm.—(Iowa poetry prize)
ISBN 0-87745-879-0 (pbk.)
I. Title: Adventures of Carlyle, my imaginary friend. II. Title. III. Series.
PS3608.A989S66 2004
811'.6—dc22   2003058385

04 05 06 07 08 P 5 4 3 2 1

To my Immortal Beloved

       without whom

I would be living naked under a bridge

The author wishes to thank the
National Endowment for the Arts for
support during a period when many of
these poems were composed and the
Wyoming Arts Council for support and
encouragement over many years' time.

(some of)

The Adventures of Carlyle,

My Imaginary Friend

selections from

Book I
  (some of) The Adventures of Carlyle, My Imaginary Friend

Book II
          (some of) The Further Adventures of Carlyle,
                    My Imaginary Friend
                      including:

                  Carlyle & the Black Pool
                   Carlyle as Cloud
                   Carlyle & Fire
                Carlyle as Surgeon/Scientist
                Carlyle as Magician/Jester
                 Carlyle & the Underside
                  Carlyle & the Book
               When Carlyle Reaches Under
                  Carlyle & the Mirror
                  Carlyle & the Edge
                  Carlyle & the Ghoul
                  Carlyle & Some Boxes
                  Carlyle Trepanning

Book III

Snippets (or:)

The Briefer Escapades of Carlyle, My Imaginary Friend

(or: Carlyle Miscellaneous)

(or: Carlyle as Adjunct)

(or: Carlyle: Fragments)

Cameo appearances by:

Ruth, the Boy, the Hag, 2 Nymphs, Astor Piazzolla, Aliens,

the Hanging Man, Ghost,

& Others

(Does not include:

Book IV

Carlyle Whole)

Carlyle can see
from the bottom of his hole, all
glorioso, strangely –

oh why –

What other
in his brown brain – fur, his
luxurient/opulous, knows more
or better, any

❖

Carlyle's garden runs a little ravaged, wild.

❖

Carlyle sings the news with soul & lip waggle –

❖

When he shakes his tail-
bone, vertebrae fly.

❖

Carlyle's contagions confound
the uninspired, vex chance –

Carlyle is spore, & mild.
He is swoon & sherbet.

❖

When Carlyle – then
Carlyle.
　　　　Crow
comes down – lugubriously –
hollers: Wrong! Carlyle! Wrong!

❖

surrounded by rock-miles
& nowhere, who
shouts — or doesn't — dozens
                                    — o, Ruth
sly, solip-
sism — schism — swag
& rosy — reclines, creaking,
sippering rue-
rum — *sorry* . . .
                        Love —
Love I was wrong.
What. a. day.
                    Jig-
skip & vanish — who
once was and still
is — sighs, and puts up her huge
white feet.
                    Carlyle shouts: Un-
lock your hair — off!
with your hat, let's begin
& end, at once.
                        Ruth, I rue . . . o,o,o

(If Carlyle is Carlyle/Ruth . . . who am I?   o,o,o)

❖

While drowning, Carlyle writes a mass.
It comes to him, all at once. The horns,
the mezzo. Or maybe it's only a motet.
There isn't much time. There's that bottom
to contend with. Boulders. Silt. Mud.
The snag. He thinks maybe he'll add
a tuba — something so far down . . .
Drone — water-gabble, rush —

❖

                         I'm here
he shouts — Here! I'm —
but the wind tears out his tongue.
All he's left with is snippets
& tattered.
                Give me a gist-
hint, Mr. C — when do we hit?

❖

Carlyle imagines a world
without food . . . without
eating, without this
constant fuss & bother —

Soon, the cave of his gut,
beneath perfectly
sprung ribs — is a hollow
space — sprung
with the darkness
of concavity, all
sparkling shimmer

consumes — ravenously — everything,
even him. O, Carlyle!

❖

Carlyle knows, too well
the ambitions of the hand.

If I think of Carlyle as boy
my black umbrella closes.

Grasped by the cracked heel, Carlyle cannot —

And after it's over?
Carlyle stacks jokes
like thunderheads.

Where is my other with whom
I moved in the womb
as one? O, how we shook;
how we made her belly
jelly-jump!
                    – where . . .
I want to take your wrist
I want to lift your hand.

We are so close, now. Almost . . . see?
that your ribs even flaming feel like mine –
your cape your wings your black mask.

refusioness delusioness
toot-toot your royal
                . . . o . . .
Carlyle flops back on his bed,
scratches his head, somehow –
somehow he's always & never – look
what a lip-flurry! faster –
than eye-light – yet
somehow I MUST seem, I must
mean . . . redeem-sheen?
Carlyle imagines the mirror
and how he puts his hand
in it – this time
he promises this time – &,
oblique-oblage, in some vague-perhaps,
some peremptory off-hand, unscrews
the top of his head.
Scary! hisses: Whoa!
little doggy, it's NOT

like everybody else's . . .
and shock-eyed walks out
holding his hank of curl
& lock, swinging
it, singing —

❖

In Carlyle's houses curtains stir.

Lounging on the couch, Carlyle
ciphers shadows, consonants,
vowels:
        Love — he whispers.

❖

          Carlyle convulses.
His body, on the bottom, makes
a rude and fleshy mark

drone & sonic whump.

❖

                             (this time)

Carlyle writes a fugue — nervy
little ditty — it goes on & on.

❖

throat-song, thrum-
hum from larynx

❖

Carlyle's on the roof:
a shingle lifting — crazed
cahoot — whatsmore
he is gradual —

whatsmore, neither greater-
than nor less – Carlyle
is the draft that stirs
curtain & dustbunny

(when all the windows
and all the doors are shut).

❖

Carlyle gums gloppy –
ruminates, cogitates,
screws up his face
and yowls. Carlyle contorts – pretzel-like –
and settles before the corpse.
                              Long ago
the eyes were plucked, rectum
hollowed, bored by beak –
keen – & eye. Carlyle pokes
at the loosening joints
with a forked stick. He doesn't mind
helping things along. *Whoo-oops!*
he chortles – all's apart, awry.
He scratches in the legholes
of his loincloth. He uncrosses
his knees, unwraps his head.

❖

In Carlyle's congregation, all the crows are pure.
                              What. a. <u>racket</u>! –
But what is all this goldness? He asks.
It is nothing – I lie – take my hand.
Leaf upon boister-
creek – red chokes . . . Why this
avatar?
          wall of yellow, well of gold –
scattered teasel & dock –
smells like the crease, that
waxy shadow behind Carlyle's extravagant ear.

Then it's the black wing, wind-cloak — *we* —
which enfolds. In its dark space, downy, warm
and secure, pressed naked length to length,

                                    my hand in his —

❖

& resumes other — some previously former
breath of brain-span and thusly, therefore

                        (Carlyle is a bridge)

❖

Now he is a troop of boy meat.
Now Carlyle root-snuffles crotch-
pocket, hem — odorous occlusion — kisses . . .

summer sun-struck, stark in brunt

❖

hiss biddy, hiss — here
comes a dream — like an army,
the red dream at dawn — wall
of fury, fire — the cubicle, the ceiling
on its rack & pinion tread
coming down, to meet the floor.
                        Blood puppy,

❖

Carlyle buys a house
with nothing in it —

really & truly, no basement, only
an open craw: hot, steamy — slick.

                    Then Carlyle
gets naked, pinches
his nose, scrunches
eyes shut and shouts:
                              here goes!

❖

Carlyle mercurial
spilled in a white bowl –
who can hold him?

❖

(in the boy's bathroom
crayoned on the wall:
Carlyle is a _____)

❖

Who but Carlyle would recognize
the pattern of its wings – sheen-shimmer –
the oily I.D. of its particular, peculiar
translucence – & call it by name?

❖

in the snow glowing orange
flame against the gray firs

before that: Carlyle holding the match,
the can of gasoline, the solid

whump! of uncontrolled ignition –
knocked to his knees, the gloved hand

smoking – eyebrows, lashes entirely
gone – Carlyle, this time we were lucky?

_____

❖

First I went down to the water –
and there were two water nymphs,
jewel shadows. A path led to,
and one went away. And when they came out
of the water, shy at having been
caught, their pale new skins,
all along the lengths of their bodies,
blushed. Then I went with one
into a room that wasn't –

Far, in a white house tucked
against – a light comes on.

(Is this my Carlyle, supping alone?
With what enormous eye has he pierced
my dreaming? Does he pity?)

❖

                                            You.
Tell me something I don't – whispers.

How I long, I long
to place my fresh face, sweet face, clean
on the pillow – sleep
through, and wake love-eyed.

❖

I know the list
& dozens. Can you
sing that? – he asks – do you
know that tune?

❖

                              – splitting
plump scale shimmer,
Carlyle pulses out.

Sloughed, the discard
crumpled in root-catch — now what
does Carlyle become? Wing
of sheer translucence,
loft — star-slung
sapphire above the dreg —
he is tenuous bone-
tones and glistening.

(What strange creatures
we might become, if we were to follow
Carlyle's exemplar.)

Now Carlyle means, without idea.

❖

Carlyle calumnious/luminous
sissing grass in the evening glass.

She is sheer marveling.
Perhaps it is Ruth   (before —)
milk smooth &
                    harmless
as rinsed light, as the thinnest
December — arc & sliver-lit.

❖

When Carlyle looks at the sun
he doesn't go blind.
He can look a long time.
                                            (if Carlyle, then Carlyle)
But when he takes his eyes back . . .

Some nights, Carlyle clamber-arcs
from our shadow-halved sphere
and flies directly, into the light.

On certain nights
with his bare eye . . .
                        Carlyle stops –
his socks fall down, his sleeves
unroll – he can see directly
into the dark parts of the moon.

(more to the point:
Carlyle can see directly into roots –
and when he comes out
he is purple-scented: lilac
in the rough wind – jostling himself)

❖

Carlyle solicitous
Carlyle caressing/addressing
drear ear –
            says with a huff:
jewel belly,
o humble
bumble-bug –
                    & pops it
into his mouth.

❖

a most peculiar
light –
        is this the light that lights
sphere-space oracular, the jelly-
disc of Carlyle's
                    eye?

❖

With his arms at lower-than
fist-hip – sprung
taughter than steel –

Carlyle considers the plunge.
With a bent knee – *sproing!*
Over the edge he goes.

❖

                        hello.
hello   canyou
see   see   can you
                              (o-o)
I love
            love

(Can you feel
my 2 hearts
                beating?)

❖

Playing the shell game
his hands move dazzler –
what he clutches
is air, and spins it.
Finding the pea, Carlyle palms it
into his mouth – explains:
                        here is the melody,
here variant – passes it, trick
coin between, over,
under gnarly bone –
                        (now you try)
and here is the drone,
its bottom, the tune or its null;
driven deep – hammered
fathoms – here is the iron
ball, the chain, the ankle hasp . . .

o no! here we go again –
                        (glug glug glug)

❖

Carlyle looking for the black pool –
glimmer in dim-day – travels
zig-jog, hackles up.
If he catches its scent,
he puts his nose to the ground,
huzz-snuffle, and goes
like a hound, waggly
and muscular.
        For he loves even
the river underground,
its terrible airless burrow –

❖

                Within
drift-curve, black birch thicket –
some come to drink and break
latticed lip with breath, some
with beak & claw – but most
to start & shy, circle
            around it.

– upon/in it –

Carlyle meets the hag
himself; and in her bag
of roots and bark, leaves
and pollen that she touches
to her forehead and sends
four ways, is every cure.

❖

                          (this time)

When Carlyle steps into the pool
he is long-limbed, white, steaming
haze-aura. When Carlyle steps into
the black pool, the bright sun spangle-

bangs against the backs of his knees –
precise, delineate – no wind
no wind! Carlyle shivers –
must I? and plunges in.
The last things showing
are his shins, the white, beautiful,
shapely soles of his feet –
                              If weeks go by
how would we know it?
Carlyle is somewhere below.

When I drag
grapple-hooks, ball
of palm smearing –

I imagine Carlyle can hear my singing,
my lullaby, my –

Now he can see the o
of my lips, melting
ice – and he will rise
through the waters, float
suspend – my fish my eel my
scutellum armored merman-amour –
and meet me, pressing
his mouth from below: o –
                              & answer.

❖

Carlyle lies like a relic.
When he rises from his slab
he steps beside the tree –

❖

Carlyle, connoisseur of breath, admits
most times it's best to resume, unless . . .
And this is where – iris-roll – he sways,
sunning the backs of his eyes.

Stayawhile –

even though the sun is moving,
even when the clouds sort through.

Meanwhile, have a bowl of soup,
a little bread and then something
sweet, a sliver of cake, tea.

❖

When Carlyle palms his eye
walking wind-crest at scuffle-
jog – turning cartwheels – & pops it
into his mouth, eyestalk
& all –
          (now you try)

❖

Arriving at storm-shore
wades out into the sea.
In the blood-tide – incoming –
driven by fishes & moon-hound –
Carlyle is foam-flecked, lashed
spume sharpening –
how his soft bones
jiggle in their purse of skin –
swell-stagger
thrall, wind-deckled
speeding of foam, roar.

When he casts his eye-bait out, setting
drag-anchor rip in sound – he feels
hand-over-hand, in his upturned palms
thrum and oscillations remotest.

❖

Astor Piazzolla has closed his eyes.
Astor Piazzolla is dreaming of Carlyle,
dancing in the sawdust, barefoot

(in his hand, the small
of a thin boy's back: it is like fire,
and rippling
              — *duende* —
& then he kisses back his eyes,
                         tenderly).

Astor Piazzolla has closed his eyes.
Wherever he goes, we will follow.

❖

Carlyle's in the attic.
He's closed the door
and nailed it shut.
Evenso, he sings
    o-o-o
holding his face.

He's chinked
all the cracks —
not even a wish
could find its way

out. In the corner
standing in shadow
is somebody known
and not. Luckily,

Carlyle is with the lunatic
(first they become
smoke, then mingle)

who believes
in continuous love
for all things.

Carlyle forms
a hoop of his hands
for the sound
to boom through.

With his arms
he makes a small
o –

If he spits, if
pucker-lipped he hawks
a pebble, out comes

My Dearest Carlyle,

How goes your long journey?
Are the rose whips
red against the blue, evening
snow? and the thorns?

                        Similarly,
here.

Carlyle, inside my curlicue
ear is a spiral –
                as you know,
also something small
and many legged, hissing.
(Is it yours – you lend it?)
It is
        like a jewel – dewy orb –

Now I think maybe I too
shall live underground, for the view
is more pronounced, and up is only.

❖

Carlyle as bigness
incarnate, tangles cloud.

His elbows – bony
protuberant contraptions – swipe.

❖

(Carlyle, when you open
clasped hands, from their hollow bowl
a fawn-colored bird luffs
out, perches on digit, sings.)

❖

                          – and here
the splendid plane
of browsnout. Where
to put the eye-
puzzle? Taking
jittery (as well as
the endless expected)
in stride, what else
should Carlyle say now
but *jimmer-stile*?

❖

Unfortunately, Ruth is in lockup.
It's a good thing Carlyle knows the way.
Ruth! he hisses.
                    – You?! –
He cuts her loose,
and by the hand,
they're out the window.

❖

rabble of bird, dour
disorder –

Then he pops me on the chin
and tries his knees – unequivocally –
Testing. testing. one two three
four – looks at me, directly
suggests: *let's jump* –

❖

effusient floresce –
everything's tender,
bruisable – wet –

❖

Black cows & bare branches
against the green, blue –
like a painting, still wet,
which suggests nonetheless
something beyond itself, and so
indeed a crow appears
& flaps – and then, rising
from behind it,
a plume of smoke: somebody –
perhaps it is Carlyle
– burning
            (and as he feeds
his little dome of flowers, flames
nearly invisible
in the bright sun,
                    he hums).

❖

cast
        cloud shadows dart, elaborate

the deep and its fishes.
                        It's a marvel.
Silt-muddle
settles . . . then the light
is like a bomb, anti-nuclear, that descends
to shelf, pressure depth-set,
and implodes.
                        Clean slate!
Clean slate! Carlyle shouts.

❖

– we're not
after all . . . So then
he straps on our lead boots
and takes my hand (his hand
is like a petal).

Shudder-rhyme – he commands –
jilt-baby: shimmer –
it's not over yet. Thusly, we step off
suspend. Remember
he says (& I do) we
are little birds now, but
incandescent.

                    (Clack
bill & hiss . . . Carlyle stretching
snaky neck, hisses back –
                        And so,
we descend, appended.)

❖

When he holds the front
of confabulatory
edge – what he sees
reflected, twitches
feint, approaches
sidewards, sidescance,

swinging. When therefore
Carlyle unhitches invisible
& whiryligigs, what he tricks
is light:
   far
peripheries, incendiary.

❖

Carlyle as Nimbus
puffs columnar.

For he is blue-black and clapped
sound, burgeoning –

For he contains shock-pulse – irregular;
For at times like these
he is hyperbolic, & garrulous.
He creates himself
daily out of gust & breeze
or, conversely, out of stillness:
sumptuously. Then again,
he slips sideways, against himself.
For the hues appear sparkler
& he is underlit,

❖

For he tucks me in, swaddled.
Luxuriate – he says – and closes
my eyes.
   (But Carlyle, o
first-&-last-formed . . .
what about the rain?)

❖

for there is light
upon the herb, fire
that breaks the shell

                    for he is
earth-rich, nurture – rain
                         wind

(& of course, he is
that sweet boy
& the kiss
neverending I thought
I'd have to steal)

❖

                                        for Christopher R.

But then he turns
inside the jewel, within
the rows of bloom –
fantastical –
and lies upon his back –

watching the rise and sudden
light – calls out – and from his vanishing
reappears.

            (That's a good trick –
Carlyle assures, and puts on his wings
like a dove.)

❖

beetle in backwash
gigs laze & spin –
changing, changing –

the sluice-stone, quavering

❖

                  this time
he has two arms
two legs & his famous
eye. But first
Carlyle takes a bow.

❖

we must muster ourselves.
                         For now,
his face is smudged.

❖

Carlyle raves wonderment/adore.

❖

Carlyle pulls at his face
which is rubbery, malleable,
and takes every shape.

Sometimes he molds a snout
& toots. Sometimes he goes so far
as to pull the bones back −
reveals: orb − how its swift
surface swirls − he huffs it
like a stone
                (*little beauty*).
                              & too
it may contain the living fire.

(also: bird and its song;
& the cloud & the pool
reflecting it; & the hoof
disturbing wrack & sheen;
& the mouth drinking
from it . . . & also
the flower, & the living
& the dead & that is why
sometimes Carlyle has to
close up his head
                or else

❖

When brain dregs
mix light & spoor –
he tells, instructs:
erase every possible
track, theme –
with a branch, or hip-
wriggled tail.

❖

Carlyle as magician/jester –

Carlyle wears cowl
& robe: the stars
the sun & the moon
on a blue ground. In one
hand: his scepter,
in the other, spinning
its own: the orb.
His face, this time, is impervious
to rain, hail, fire.
When comets scud
or the sickle moon
swipes, or when a sun
implodes – these seem
to leave no mark.
Already, Carlyle is
scarred enough
                    & bears it.

❖

                    One day
it's Carlyle this Carlyle
that – until he grabs my mouth
in his hand & squeezes –
with a thumb in one cheek-
socket and a fuck-me finger

in the other – shakes
until my marbles begin to roll
a little bit and I can feel all that
blood, stoppered up in my head.

                         (off we go)

Hey. You –
               somebody shouts –
what's going ON up there?

I know a thick plume
spouts, and then, briefly, a vague
perfume, with something like
kerosene at the bottom
                         of it. Hush
Sonatina, Carlyle soothes –
(for this is my assumed, the second
name I wrote in public
at the ball, in my tux, earlier,
wearing my eyes) (I was belle
& penchant; I was ravishing)

. . . Carlyle is beginning
undo. He is skilled, practiced.
And then I see his fingers go
like snakes, incredibly –
thin & glassy/opalescent,
                         probing,
nosing their way through
my skin my
sternum – and if there is any
doubt I don't feel it, not even when eventually
he has to crack bone & – splintery
rib stubs –
               parts me.

               Go ahead
I say, if that's what you want.

(He eats it like an apple.)

Someone has lit the candle —

someone known
& not & Carlyle
curls around it
like a fireproof
cat in the crook
& snores all night
until it gutters.

A certain glaze
of acrobatic light —
chuff-stutterer, orange
quaver — flares
across the walls.

(The boy sleeps on.)

In cloud-
scurry, crest-curve: arc
of plume: moon-swept:
                rising —
Carlyle as only Carlyle
can, sings spit-huzzle —
like a droplet
hawked into smoke.

(Now the boy is on his back,
sheets twisted around his hips —
he is like a statue; he might as well
be made of marble — with one arm
thrown across his eyes — which Carlyle

gently removes, plucks
                              like roses.
The plane of his chest —
even his nipples
which are small, and puckered —
is white; even his navel, which is a hollow
thimble of flame.)

❖

With a nostril-reed poked
up from the bottom, Carlyle
tastes of the fumes.

❖

Today, when he emerges —
his wings are fire,
curtains of explosive,
                              and his toes
are splayed flames
leaping:
          10 blue plumes   (like little soldiers)
spouting hiss
each step he takes.
Today Carlyle singes
the hair of the rabbit —
at extreme speed, hurtling
inertic.
          And from the snake
he takes its skin,
leaves it underlayer-bone,
pith-white.

❖

This time, I am the Snow Queen —

my thigh laid longways besides: pure
white: alabaster. This time I am carved

& hewn – statuesque – permanently
poised – symbol of oncemeant – that jars
occlusion, remind. Meanwhile, Carlyle,
black as nugget-meat, crispy,
curls crackle as we rub.
And when his skin sloughs
smatter-tatters, ribboned – underneath
is the blue we've been looking for –
like the inside of a shell – like the pearl.

❖

He listens
with his knees which are bent
like a tuning fork

Then he makes a noise
                          after
(like a train).

What he straddles
(besides wind   this time,
& noise)
          is discharge

(effluvial).

❖

Carlyle exotical
shows off his blue skin –
wraps his arms – spiral
band – around
thighs to ankle-hasp.
Then he turns
slowly, gravityless
in arc & wind –
somersaults – above the couch,
in the little room.

❖

Carlyle as dragon-
fly, lights a little fuse,
blue tipped: (

)

    And then
it's the amazing concussive
whoosh.
    Look –
Carlyle says, jubilantly –
watch
    my paper wings!

❖

What is this heap
of ash? Shall I
      stir it
with digit & poking
find ember & bone?
Shall I wet my thumb
and taste of it?

❖

& then he hears it – knell
in a tin bowl: reverberation
without end

❖

& then he puts his smirk on
There! he says – how's THAT for size?
(let the crickets begin triumphant)

❖

He raises his baton –
with the pencil nib
screwed into the end –
& begins. It comes

to him allatonce of a piece –
the basses and baritones with their trembling
& dread – then: ethereal
                              plaint.

❖

And when he has shown
them each
              perfected/reflected
its own face

then he takes out a mirror
(because he has others, & plenty)
& breaks it.

❖

At cock's crow
Carlyle climbs the rise of tin –
sucker-toes splayed,
unimperilled – squats
next to the weathervane
spinning wildly.

❖

When the cricket stops
what ear begins?

❖

                              slows
in the cold bowl – icy

glissade – it's the low
tones he favors, craves –

                    quavery wail –
the ring as we rub sharp-edged
the rim of a glass with wetted

                    thumb.

❖

now – even before he wakes
Carlyle stoppers up his head –
all seven orifices – drives
the bungs

          home – Now
he says, NOW I can.

❖ ❖ ❖

Carlyle & the Underside

Carlyle loves
the undersides of things –
for example:
the back of the boy's knee –
where sweat might puddle,
& Carlyle could
lap it like a cat.

& the bottom of the bowl
& the underside
of fire – where sticks meet – where
color begins.

Carlyle loves the underside –

of bridges – the shadowy
linger, all day
under – the reflected
spangle that darts up

                    into —
he loves the whirlpool
at the abutment's edge &
the body that plummets

❖

When Carlyle looks at the underside
of a leaf —
            then again
the underside of a rose —
even the idea of the underside of the rose . . .

❖

Carlyle is terrified of the underside
of the snake — although he loves it, too.

What he can't stop
thinking about; what he keeps
remembering — is the blue
arc sizzling in the space between
its belly and his hand.

Then he has to keep
the idea of it, like
sloughed skin, in a jar
on the windowsill — in light
after light has bleached it
sheer. Carlyle takes a match
& lights it, holds it
                    on this side.

❖

(If I killed the snake
and threw it
on the domed
cone — gravel,
ash & bits —

they would eat it,
regardless.
They would trot its eyes out
from its sockets
into the bole – and they would savor
its tongue, fleshy
wag, for what it used to say –
as for its skin,
they would favor
white underpinnings – underlayer –

                                        pith.)

❖

                              This time
when he offered the boy a rose
already it was bleeding –
and now it is a lotus in the heartbowl
– brookfire & cloudfeathers –
The root of the rose is farther
underside, than any imagine.

❖

Inside the underside
what compromise
confounds compose?
You need not specify! – Carlyle cries.
                    Carlyle cries:
Give me a gist-hint,
inkling.
            If Carlyle

❖

Carlyle, create suppose –
conjecture what-if. Say
sometimes – say this time, say –

What arcs
in the underside of wire & where
exactly?

I myself
love the underside
of the dog –

after he has turned
belly up –
            then too.

I myself
            – Carlyle says
fists on hips –

love the underside
of a question.
                  No?

I myself prefer the underside
of yelling – where over-
tones, lead-heavy, drop.
They make a noise like a hole
in the ground, at your feet –
like a hornets' nest.

❖

                                             for Charlie O.

Carlyle escorts the dead.
He exacts a promise.
He is the underlayer

between the bottom of the box
& the ground – cooler,
the color that receives
the wailing & the dread
from above – wet

with our tears, he is
that space that compacts
most densely
                 – after –

❖

In the underside of the vulture's wing –
In the underside of the vulture's jowl,
wedged in dewlap, is a bit of flesh.

Wedged in the vulture's blood-preen
                                  is a song –

❖

When Carlyle can see
his breath – when he holds the cloud
of expelt – sphere –
between his palms – when he can hold its shadow
– when he is both the shadow itself
and that which casts light around it –
                              (when Carlyle, then Carlyle)

❖

Today (Carlyle confides) I can't FIND
the fucking underside. And then he takes
from its chain the ball (black, iron –
I couldn't have lifted it, even if
there had been 3 of me) & spins it,
grins at me, very pleased with himself.

Is it *there?* I ask –

pointing at the top of his finger, the bottom
of the ball. Smoke & stench
are beginning to issue forth. And that's when
Carlyle's face drops. And then he pulls his finger

out from under. We think it would have
gone all the way to China, except that
core of molten magma it was associated with

                              stole it back.

❖ ❖ ❖

                            − exquisite.

Like a worm in the bone
                   then it goes
forward on suction feet.
All it wants to do, is eat.

It is like a humped-up
wave, tunnels sinusway −
makes a noise like a roar
with no excuse − needed.
It knits the eye shut.

     (. . .)

Better wrap it in light − spin a nerve
sheath, soft cocoon. Later −
it will shake its wings out.

What if the wing
that clasps & sheathes is pure
fire? Carlyle,

when I come through
to the other side, with long strides −
and my hair is gone −

my eyelids − I am pure
bone, sockets . . . then

will I terrify?

❖

If it is a daytime she imagines
in the slur preceding –
                                    then the bees drift in
golden, undetermined
arcs – alight.

                                        (*Amen* –
                        Carlyle intones, head bowed.)

❖

or he is the boy – angled
into wedge – smooth –
with his eyes at half-hood
as the lights tick on.

❖

facing each & each – bare
feet touching arch on arch

. . . even the figure passing through – would not unlock their eyes

❖

not even almost-as-
if – but truly, he enters
what once seemed
closed as an echo –

with his night-eyes on:
darting, wheeling –
                                entangles.

❖

              (this time)
Carlyle makes
a line of fire across the sky –

segment of arc

❖

(& of the 16 dead alighted,
they make a pox in the sky)

❖

Sometimes Carlyle forgets how
to put his hands when he sleeps – where
to put his wrists & elbows

decides: THIS is the place to investigate.
And so he turns.
And if his ankle twitches & spasms
again – just as he's dropping off –
it's because of the hasp, the chain.
[   ]
I'm not an angel, yet.

❖ ❖ ❖

                              Carlyle & the Book &
                  When Carlyle Reaches Under

(Carlyle opens the book, desultorily.)

❖

When Carlyle opens the book, birds fly out.
They look like letters in disguise   – either

❖

epiphanies alight, ever so briefly, preen –
& then it's all out the window
tout-de-suite & I don't mean maybe

      they're GONE.

❖

But when I open the book . . .

❖

All the children are amazed
because my name appears with the dead.
They throng & clutter the sidewalk
touching me, touching –

❖

When Carlyle reaches under – brilliant
pincers tick-tick-ticking –

      what he nabs
right off, is Dust Bunny
who then weeps: real, golden tears.
So Carlyle puts it back.

I suppo-o-ose . . . he hums, scratching
his head, with that claw
leaving a groove, curve-complaint, a crease –
and then he reaches under again

❖

When Carlyle reaches under, it is like
the black bag he totes – sack of uncertain
proportion; in fact, it grows huger
by the minute as Carlyle rummages

through – elbow, shoulder, neck-
deep.
  Eventually
when he comes up for air
which he has to, what he drags
behind him at stretched-arm
length, is a carcass, fairly fresh,
with the blood scarcely dry,
& the tatters & the ruins.

Then Carlyle picks his teeth
– brilliantly, pearled
     orbs –

❖

& yes, that time one time he reached in
& pulled out a comet
    whole & entire.
You can only imagine proximity/perplexity
(not to mention hiss)
    how it smote –

And so it is when Carlyle jots
ephemera – conjectures – when he sketches elliptical

❖

(And then he gets out his compass &
draws the first arc.)

❖

When Carlyle reaches under
     this time
what he catches, what he nabs
by snarl & lock
   is the witch-bitch.
Broom-bones, sticks – she is full

of spiel & incantation.

— Alas —

Carlyle says — she loves the ends of things
too well — & so, is forced

to let her go.

❖

for Sam W.

The last time Carlyle reached under
what he grabbed was a premise. Worse:
it was still alive. Worse yet: it tried to bite back.
When he did finally and with great force
throw it back — it set up such a howl
that it woke up Ruth (who was completely
ensconced); who then went after it on all fours
— a real knockdown dragout until, finally
Ruth biffed it on the nose & it was
out for the count. It's possible
they're down there still. By now, who knows
what # she's come to?

next time
next time

❖

When Carlyle builds a stairwell —
the better to get all of himself
under — he builds it at spiral
with jewel-pickets

❖

When Carlyle reaches under a star
what he catches is light, & later.
The far peripheries . . . he cups
in his hand & holds to his ear.

❖

– preceding.

When Carlyle reaches under a star
what he catches is blackness
& null – then he tugs at its tail.

❖

When Carlyle reaches under
what he catches is stray – sinewy –
bigger than his hand
can hold, and turns back on itself.

❖

All glories in the fallen
light – including Carlyle

who does magnify
not only golden
but the umber, &
the backlit crow.

❖ ❖ ❖

(Instantly, the dream is forgotten.)

When Carlyle walks around it
with his arms behind his back,
wrists crossed, his hands
fluttery as jittertail, or a dance,
what he sees is both sides
                            at once.
And so he lights a candle and sets it

(exalted it appears
                    both
same & altered
throughout).

                              – smudged –

and then from behind his right ear:
a rhythmical breathing
                              – who rests
in this glowing, nape upon nape?

Carlyle, feel its bone.

❖

When the light hits
skew & burrows –

❖

Carlyle sits like a jewel
in the middle of the pool
cross-legged on a rock.

If his eyes are open
or closed – it's impossible
to tell, because of the light
that comes from behind & around
the corner – and bathes him
                              golden.

❖ ❖ ❖

                                        Carlyle & the Edge

When Carlyle muckles onto
the edge –

When he grabs the edge by the blade
& swings it –

When Carlyle yells at the edge,
nothing maunders
                    echoes/answers
back – for the sound accelerates
like a marble on a tilted mirror.

                                        —————

When Carlyle yells at the edge
his mouth seems especially
                              tender –
his voice rushing
both over & under
                      allatonce.

❖

                          after
Carlyle has grabbed
the edge – for a very long time –
what he leaves behind
is a smudge, a greasy
lingering – bright
red – that dries
from the perimeter
                      inwards.

❖

When Carlyle holds the edge
to his eye – one
lash-width away –

❖

                      also,

it is like a guillotine –
& those moments
                  after –

blinking in the light.

❖

Carlyle at the edge
of precipice, refuses.

It's too far down
to manglebone. Isn't that it?
Isn't that the tune?

Carlyle sings La La La.

When Carlyle steps to the edge –

it's sheer all the way & besides
Carlyle nods – Ruth may
or may not be
waiting at the bottom
with a sheet spread out.
                    Evenso

if Carlyle had a trumpet he would toot the charge . . .

That's when the boy
calls out, HEY! did you forget about me?

Because the boy is beautiful beyond measure;
because most everyone guesses distance and plummet
                                        wrongly
Carlyle surrenders. Then the boy
throws a look, whereupon Carlyle
does more than surrender, he dives.

Sometimes, when Carlyle staggers down

        after a long, bad night
        & turns on the light
                        he discovers
a veil between
            himself & the bright
                        edge
(like cellophane, yellow sun-stained)

(like a second eye-
lid – membrane – & so,)

❖ ❖ ❖

Carlyle & the Ghoul

When Carlyle can't decide
(what Carlyle CAN?) – that's
a good time to call.

He'll be sitting there
                              on the edge
of his bed, rubbing
the bare soles of his feet together
– furiouser & furiouser –

            Furtively
he glances
at the window to see,
is the ghoul still there.

                    (Now
would be a good time   .
to call, because Carlyle would jump
10 feet into the air, maybe more,
straight up & exclaim:
                              THAT's a good trick!)

What Carlyle can't decide
is whether or not –
                    the light –
because of the light, he thinks –
beating against the glass,
incessantly – it keeps.

What Carlyle can't decide
in his mind which won't

rest easy, which can (or cannot, quite)
imagine what the ghoul

                        might do –

what Carlyle can't decide about
are the consequences, whether or not
his chances might have

                            improved.

                        If only
                        this time
                        today
tonight what he can't decide about,
can't bring himself to think about

❖

What Carlyle can't decide
is whether he should get up
and walk across the room

                        (& turn off the light)
                or not.

❖

What Carlyle can't decide about

                            this time
is whether or not the glass
will shatter, if he presses his forehead
against it, very hard.

❖

When Carlyle opens the book he knows the ghoul
from the window, is watching over his shoulder.

Even rill & tremor-fear, the yodel
at the back of Carlyle's throat
does not move – it.

                              – Bah! Carlyle
snorts & returns to his work.
He picks up his choicest
tool (from the stack beside the book)
shiny, sharp –
                    & begins to cut arcs
(like cookies, as if he were a baker making
scrumptious) into the sheer
translucence of his book.

                    Today –
                              he says, ignoring the ghoul,
we'll measure the Abyss –

& reaches for his rule.

                                        Tonight
the ghoul is at the window again
when Carlyle opens the book.
                              This time
its black face
is pressed against the black pane
like night, only
without any of the stars behind it.

                                        Next time
Mr. Ghoul, Carlyle warns, shaking
his finger at it – You
will be in, for a big surprise.

And then he slides
surreptitiously, with his wrist
like rubber – a tool
from his favorite stack
into the drawer of his desk, & another
he stuffs up his sleeve.

So there – he says,
leaning back in the chair, crossing
his knees, looking up

                              – whistling
with his cheeks puffed-out big,
bright as balloons,
his forehead beginning to bead
with effort.

              (That's when
the ghoul cracks a little smile.)

❖

                              (one time)
                              (this time)
When the ghoul isn't
looking, Carlyle changes into
a snake – with shaky
skin, fangs – sidewinds back.
                              Ho! –
Carlyle yells – look out
                    little fella –
& that's when he smells the incense,
hears the pipe
& fluting keen.
              Mesmerized
Carlyle flares his cowl,

because the mouthpiece of the horn
is engulfed by the ghoul;
it has its whole face behind it
all-encompassing . . .

& the brass bell
is inches, a lash-width, away from
Carlyle's eye.

                         (Someday,
Carlyle says, he promises – I will swing from it, like a clapper.)

❖

                    This time
when Carlyle opens the book
what he finds inside
– much to his chagrin –
is the ghoul, very flat, 2D,
like a rose . . .

❖

What Carlyle finds
when he opens the door of his little room
is Ruth –

she has her mouth full   (this time)
with joviality, which she hawks
up like a stone – & the boy –

his wings are folded
because they are so big, so
splendid, how else could he come into?

(What they don't know about
but Carlyle can clearly see –
is the ghoul, standing right behind.)

❖

               This time
when Carlyle opens the door
to his little back room (the one w/o
windows, doors, etc) what he finds,
with its toes curled, yellow
nails dug into
             the threshold
is the ghoul, grinning.

Its eyes are so
big, entirely
without pupil.

[If it ever had
hair, Carlyle can't tell – but its skull –
(Carlyle reaches out as if to stroke it
for luck, but draws back, in
the nick-of-time) is glossy-
smooth, black & forms
a perfect arc.

           What could be inside   (that spinning)?]

❖

What Carlyle finds – just outside

is a guest never invited.
How to entertain? Cards? –
he asks, slipping
trumps up his sleeve.
He keeps a straight face.
Sit. Please.

❖

                    This time –
when Carlyle opens the door
of his little room, what he finds, full-length, is
a mirror at cant – he can see
all of himself, allatonce –

There. See. Now What
Have You Done? – The ghoul
would say, from behind
it . . . if it had speech.

❖

When Carlyle opens the door –
what he finds
           this time
is the book.

He can't imagine
what force, or oversight,
what
could have left it
there   outside
(on purpose).
          And then, out of the shadows:
the shadow of the ghoul
distincts itself
          – hunched –
all that Carlyle can see
are the twin ridges of its spine
& the arc of its upraised
buttocks as leaning on elbows,
chin in one upturned palm –
darker darkness against the dark –
it is turning the pages

with its unopposable
thumb –

❖ ❖ ❖

Carlyle on edge
makes a rectangle, a flatness –

First he is opaque –
pane of vague remove,
within beyond – then he remains
          – pulsing –
(how he fades
and gathers himself) –
          evenso
the edge is clear, delineate.

When Carlyle grabs the edge
with fingers splayed, damp palms
skidding, thumbs apposite to, what he holds
          this time

is the mirror, which he then proceeds
to drag
        across the yard –

When Carlyle leans
over it, he has to take his face back, or lose it, forever –
& when he lies down beside it & gazes – angle-
glance – and a cloud passes over

❖

When Carlyle passes over –
sinuously –
intricate imbricate –
and I look up –
his belly is white.
When Carlyle passes over – slowly –
he is the belly of the snake without.

Horizon to horizon – entire –
he is more than line. If I reached up –

❖

(no birds no birds – the singer flies)

❖

                    – though
he sticks his finger in his ear, up to
the second bone – still
he can hear her sing.
        He thinks
she never stopped, all night long –

        Sometimes
when he shakes his head
            muscularly
like the swimmer emerging – or

like a cat that never wanted
                              in, in
the first place —
                    as if he meant
to shake the sound — out —
all he hears is where
he's already been — pressure
popping drum — or
where he hasn't thought to go
but inklings — through it all, evenso
always, that one

(that he loves & wishes)
                          sings on

❖

In Carlyle's palace

which only he inhabits —
and it is vast — when he walks
he walks with his hands
at half-mast
— & in the floors are hidden
doors; he never knows
when one, sprung —
will eat him — or where
he will be spit out,
and in what state of chew.

❖

When Carlyle turns in the earth like a worm
& comes back up, what he finds is the bird.

❖

shrouded — within
voluminous

within luxurious –
Carlyle's pelt deflects

❖

                              his breath,
his song is like a forge
at full-fire.

This is not a thing of sticks
or elemental –

and yet Carlyle arises, emerges levitate –
with his arms at Rainbow
mast, his glance:
                    rapturous.

❖

                        (sometimes)
Carlyle's ear is like a snail shell:
spiraled, many-shaded white.

When he blows across
emptiness, it will sing back
like a sackbut.

❖

What he calls forth,
& they land like a cape,
are the crows –
up to the neck in them:

black ruff –
as they jostle
& complain.

❖

He makes of himself a gnome –

He makes for himself
a home in the bole-heart
of fir, & there, inside
rot, among duff, he lays
his head in powders – ant-chew –
& snores. Not even the bird knocking
grub from bark can wake him;
neither the squirrel; nor
the lion, slobbery,
licking at the soles of his feet
where they stick out through
                              the door.

Carlyle sleeps on, harmless.

❖

In Carlyle's universe, the stars
are inured to speculation –
When Carlyle takes a stroll
through his universe
with his hands folded
behind his back – see
how they make an L
for love? – with his cheeks
puffed out he is whistling
in the dark a tune
nobody ever heard before,
but with which, after – all
will become enchanted.
Where loop-de-loop delusions
                              are revered
is Carlyle's home. It perches
on the edge of a throne,
at his right hand.

❖

questions, conjunctions/
confusions Carlyle wrestles
to the ground. What they need
is a BATH. So Carlyle gets out
his scrub brush, his bar
of soap, tub of lye.
I'm going to clean things UP –
sharpens his claws.

❖

                       (sometimes)
                      (Carlyle thinks)
I must be made of straw
& bluster. One little huff . . .
                    (one little match)

❖

When Carlyle takes my hand
& we walk out – I cannot see
where to put my feet. We go
to the gate, & open it & swing it
wide & set it onto its hooks – so that
whatever wants to come in: may.

❖

                            sometimes
when I'm holding Carlyle's hand
on the pillow by my ear –

       like a bundle of thrown
sticks –

just before, or slightly after

❖

If I had an eye
in the palm of my hand

& held it up
above my head, would it go out
shining into the night?

❖

First he passes through birds
who clutter the air. It takes
a long time — because of their wings
& their song; he is blind
until he reaches the bottom
which is immense. And there
is the river — in darkness —
to which he steps cautiously.
Because it does not reflect, he takes
deep draughts, noisily.
And because he does not need
to come up for air, he pushes
his face into it — until his earholes
fill. And then he listens
for its full endless length —
& to the drone-source,
                              constancy.

❖

                                        This time —
& so, spinning like a top, he bores
towards core, eternal
                    heart —
which is pulsing (jumper-jolt)
like a bat in a sack upside
down — slick &
                    marvelous.
                         o —

_____

he throws up his hands
in despair:
                    the possibilities
(. . .) it's the last, lasting,
that overwhelms.

❖

                    Sometimes
when Carlyle pours water
what erupts is spark,
dimple in ruffled-crest: sample,
a start.

❖

that's when
Carlyle concludes omit.

❖

Rather than
                    being horrified
Carlyle declares: now THIS
is something to investigate.

He does not throw his hands up
into the air & exclaim, but bends
& slips his finger between
                              & inside
circles encircling:
the bracelet, the hasp –
it's not raw yet.

And then the boy whimpers – wakened
by Carlyle's solicitous touch –
& twists against the rock.
                    Easy –
Carlyle soothes:
                    Think again, consider
your skin.

(That's when Carlyle dabs at his lips.)

❖

        Let's assume
the Void.
That would be the place
between &
         then some,
Carlyle adds.

❖

                     Instead of
delicacy & nuance, sometimes
Carlyle wants to clobber

& I don't mean
maybe – what he wants to use
is a 20 lb. maul.
         Lookout!

And that's when the ghoul
begins to shake in his boots
a little bit – the ones
with the upturned toes & the bells
that begin to jangle.

It is like a warning screwed to the door.

❖

Carlyle screws in the bolts
one on either side
of his neck. Now he is ready
for the lightning.

❖

Spartan in the red aisle —
wall within wall —
it's the inner sanctum
Carlyle trowels smooth.

He has built it
stone by stone
of accretions, accumulations — jewels.

What he can't discover
is the height of things.
Too, there is the problem of the ceiling.

Stone on stone —
amalgamation . . . aggregates, jewels —
it's the sparkle in his huff
he builds on.

Too late
            Carlyle thinks about
a door . . .

❖

Carlyle says *I think I shall*
confiscate your dream & with that
begins to explore.

❖

Why, you're just like the ghoul —
Carlyle says — everywhere I turn,
there you are.

❖

When Carlyle holds the moon in his arms
like the disc he wishes it was — wafer . . .

❖

Carlyle is naked
             down to the loins.
His feet are bare
             horn & dusty
the nails thick,
           golden.

❖

& if it so happens as
               sometimes
it does, that one is stirred
by something greater than,
                then Carlyle
shuffles to the top of the hill
                 & yells
to get the sound out.

❖

When Carlyle takes
              the dead from the cart
stacks them
(the soldiers, leaning on their swords,
        are weary, and impatient)

           & gently
smoothes
       remove

               it is with some anxiety
that Carlyle gets to the next.
           Lastly, because
                  what if . . .
should he come to –
        how fond I've become –

❖

                    Carefully
(pitiless, merciful)
                    under
the hot sun, the blue sky,

❖

When Carlyle alights on the steps
                            having come from the dead –
his great wings
            rising like a ridge of furl –
                                    luffing –

❖

When Carlyle lands with a thump
                            & tumbles
            with a great todo
            – all the dead are amused.

❖

When Carlyle floats   (under
                                             the bridge)
like a leaf in the stream –
                    he has that
far-away – dreamy.

Then he has to look up at
                    the underside:
light shafts dowse
eddy & whirl

as he exits
            out from under, into
(unobstructed)

❖

Savagely, his people go forth –
with the knives

(on all 4s
           it is
the bare arch of sole that thrills,
                 Carlyle concedes –
for the boy is among them,
grimy, sweaty – dirt
collected in kneepockets.

❖

On slickery –

On slow days, Carlyle dusts
the treads.
           If he makes it
all the way, he's not
about to tell.

❖

                 Sometimes
Carlyle dreams
                 longingly
of sleep while he sleeps.

❖

Carlyle cants his head
like a crow, measuring sky.

❖

When Carlyle rolls forward
                           & over
something else moves –

it is like a growth, &
undiagnosed, rolls
shank to shank & settles
                    in his belly
loose in skin, slippery-
thick,
        encased.

❖

Then, when the darkness comes
with the hollow wind –

then Carlyle heads for shelter,
making a duckwalk across
the lawn –
                fast.

❖

Ruth says: *They're back.*

Next thing you know
                    Carlyle's killing it –
He has emptied the place
                    where its eyes ought to be
with a scoop gouge.
                    Then Carlyle begins to weep,
huge, wracking sobs.
                    It's all Ruth can do
to endure it.

She has her eyes
            closed.
She has her face turned up, towards –

❖

Carlyle
        transparent

as a tune
        (nevermind
up-under
        in –)
             this time
             this time
is making of himself
a small thing
        (so as not
to interfere).
           For now

❖

What *about* evil? Carlyle asks.
How transparent
        is that?

❖

we want the clear
        high tone
stretched out long –

❖

KaBAM – Carlyle says, & extends
his hand. He's got a hoot & holler
in his fist –

When Carlyle extends
        munificence –

❖

putting his ear to the ice
like a suction cup

he wants to hear the latest
        stir
(unreliable, unverified)

What? How's that?

❖

That boy's a little ditzy –
Carlyle says. *Love*, look how flagrantly
he dreams.

❖

Carlyle says: let's not talk
                                into the darkness.
And then it's as if he has
                                extended himself.
Then he could hear
                        all the music
                                    allatonce.

❖

With his blunt probe
separating, Carlyle points out
gristle, vein, bone.

We have opened
                    the back of a hand.
It is like –

Only this time
                    this one is alive
& the anesthetic
                    is about to wear off.

Won't he be horrified? Carlyle asks
to see the bands & clamps, screws?
Won't he be horrified
                        to look up
& see us with our masks on?

❖

& the snow
clabbered in twist-knot, & the limb
loosening in the quick

❖

When Carlyle walks out into
                              the not-yet
soft, new-fallen . . .

(barefoot) – it is because
                              no one will wake.

He has shaken
                   them, in their beds;
he has beaten the bell –
                              excited, & ignored.

They sleep on.

Before him
he has only the path
                        overladen
to step off into –

❖

How small
            shall I make myself?
Carlyle wonders
                  fearfully.
When do I disappear?

❖

When Carlyle pushes against the dark
               it pushes back –

like sumo-wrestlers –
they try to grab each other
by the fat-side, hank-of-hip,
a fistfull of slick, greasy –
& throw each other.

❖

(Like a wind
upon the throne – in the crown –
Carlyle sits
            magisterially.)

❖

I was WRONG – Carlyle
effuses – it all happens
                    allatonce.

❖

On the edge
of hallucinatory dispatch –

❖

                    incipient –

under
other-lit, edge
                    – left to right –
looking for clues:
                    a hair
ribbon-flake,
sheet of skin – ream
of evidence
            (Ruth says:
It's not those damn aliens again, is it?)

❖

& the moon was with me both ways
Carlyle said —
                in the early going away
& in the middle &
                coming back.

❖

He's about to have an opinion,
                & is sorry.

❖

                        This time
when Carlyle looks under
                        the bridge
what he finds is a body

without its head: neckbones
& bloodstump
                its front
shoulder immersed —
& the ice closing in,
& allaround it
                the white snow.

❖

It is the dark
                blowing back
into itself.

❖

Laid out on a slab
beneath a heap of white flowers
(no one can see him smile)

❖

              floating
on the sea, beneath
the moon, borne inside/on
a raft of inflorescence

❖

              dimensionless
Carlyle suspends
          2 realms.

         Having to lean
farther over
        to see under
        than ever
before,

❖

                              (this time)
as he has now
        for days
Carlyle languishes –

in a small boat.
He has his feet up
         on the thwarts.
Even the undersides
of his soles are burnt, blistering –
maybe even bones show.
By day the flies swarm.
By night the fishes
         stand up
on their fins
     & gawp.

His swollen tongue protrudes

                                   amassed

through
the gate of his broken lips.

❖

                                             if, then.

Carlyle says – I should tuck & fold
attend
        this wound this
mutilation.

❖

When Carlyle hears
                 the calling of his name –

insistent, urgent
by timbre & frame
the way its vowels
             fit in the case,
drawn out,
           it's either
Ruth, the boy, the other, or a way out/
                       from

– then he wakens from his dream
& walks towards it, anyway.

❖

but the fit of it, the idea of it
                   seems a little small.

It is – he decides – like a straitjacket
that one has grown accustomed to.

Then it's time to shrug out
                        using those
collapsible shoulders –

❖ ❖ ❖

                                    Carlyle & Some Boxes

When Carlyle puts his ear
                        in that box
what he hears –

(indistinct as further
weeping)

❖

Open – he mumble-hums,
                & does.

Inside
        is the shadow of the wing.
Quick! Carlyle shouts
& slams it shut.

❖

                        This time
the box is an octagon
                        & would hold
a hat perfectly –
                without the head;
or a very large
                head, without the hat.
Either way
            Carlyle tightens the bands
& slings the whole
                    contraption
across his shoulders

(like a scout, a hiker,
like a soldier about)

❖

Having crawled into
the box, after
first having pulled it out
                        from under –
Carlyle nods:
Close it.
            Shoulders,
hips disjointed
                    he has the usual
chains crossing
& cinched under –
                    he is curled around
the ball, big as an anchor.

All right – comes the muffled
                            command –
throw me over.

❖

                    This time
when Carlyle opens the box
it is filled with water –
                    so he reaches in
with his bare hand

(he's groping for a star
or at least something
                    smooth & closes
hoping)

but when he takes his hand
                        out,
all he sees is the loveline of his palm.

❖

                              This time
when Carlyle opens the box –
with the sun
behind him, arcing
over shoulder, throwing
                        beam, shaft:
a perfect parallelogram
of clearly delineate edge –

what he sees is the bottom
of the boy, upturned –
                        rosy.

❖

If he should open
the box with his thumbs
                        imbedded
(spritz & sugar-sizzle)

❖

Had he tinkered –
                  if only –
he should have
improved closure
                  (or
with a file adjusted
by increments)

❖

When he opens the box
the ghoul pops out
                  (wearing his funny hat
                  with 3 bells on – jangle)
on his double-helix
                  spring – bobs.

❖

Opening the box
                Carlyle discovers
(is reacquainted with)
the jewel – nestled in velvet –

❖

When Carlyle pokes at the lid
                        gingerly –
because he has this feeling,
or maybe it's just the hinges
                        glowing –
[   ]

then Carlyle knows his eyebrows are gone;
and when he rubs his cheek
down to the bone, farther –
ashes fall in heaps, mounds

❖

First he pulls out snuggle-bunny: white –
then a porcupine & finally at long last –

❖

                Wonders
if he oughtn't to
                sit in it.

And then the box sprouts wings.
It is like a chariot, decides –
                        climbs in.

❖

o! Maker of things – boxes,
birds & wings,

music
like a rhyme-crown, daisy
chain, ring –

(
)

o Maker of things!

(& if it's wrought –)

❖

bodily
dragging forth.)

One foot hooked –
both braced on either edge   (of the box)
Carlyle looks down, into.

This time – then –
This time, first –

– framed & backlit –

This time, that –   (lastly)
as opposed to

(in the middle in particular)

This time, without –
increasingly

❖

This time, it isn't
bottomlessness
that assaults –
but the idea underneath.

The box within the box
                    swings up on
articulated hinge: a separate
                         lift-out tray.

              Ingenious —
Carlyle admits.

❖

When the moon fell
                    out of the orange
                                   sky
then Carlyle's city began to burn:
                         everything
nearer

❖

I said: quick!
              the moon
is falling out of
              the eastern sky.

All of this happened (increasingly)
                         a long time ago —
& Carlyle has kept it, all this while
                    safely
locked in the box (one of his many)
                         even though
he knows its containment
is from the world before
                    & after —

and it is only in this little, this briefest
that Carlyle can know
                    about the hiding place
of the key.

(either. He will tell us
or not.)

❖

This particular
                    box, has holes
                              drilled into its sides
(because the creature inside
                         requires immediate −)
                                             & slots
for its wings.

❖

But Carlyle has this one
                         attached to a string
so that the farthest
                    it can go, is into

❖

                    inside
this particular box
is a bowl −
& floating in the bowl
is a flower −
& inside the flower
is a stone −
& inside the stone
                    unreleased
is the flame.

(& inside the flame −)

❖

When Carlyle pulls
                    on opposite sides
of the box − a hatch

flickers spatial break, sliding – &
a man pops out
arms splayed – wide – as if
a wire, extremely
                    tensile,
curved out
from his breast . . . as if
a hook
         imbedded –

And his eyes . . . o!
he is still
          alive.

                                        (Carlyle is sorry
                                                      sorry

❖

in the morning, warning in the white
box – is the cricket, coal baby, nugget
of soot – black, raking shiver-song.

❖

When Carlyle considers
the quarters, the question –
(he ends up) confounded/
dumbfounded – jubilant.

❖

Because sorrow skewed corners –

                    when Carlyle clambers into
the box, this time
                    (delicately, he
weighs like a feather, softly – wearing his freshest –

because he knows, he remembers, something about
                                                    pressure & breakage

❖

Inside the mirror-box – milk-
lit, in its swirling –

Carlyle on hands & knees, sees
all of himself allatonce
                            exposed – groping.

It's the bony vowels he's looking for
                                                    (this time).

❖

Of Carlyle's conjectures, one must infer
                                    conclude, a certain
mirth, untied tongue-
waggle, lip-horn
                        trumpeting –

❖

Carlyle lives in
                singular –
windows all around.

It is like a watchtower.

He is above the crow, higher.

❖

Having caulked all the seams
& waited for them to cure
Carlyle yells
                fillerup!
This box

is tall as a tower
the kind with signs
& razor-wire tangling
                    perimeter,
lights all night long
& men with machine guns
patrolling.
                Fillerup!
Carlyle yells, once more.

He has his hand
                hovering
above the red button –
twitchy – because he knows
as soon as the starship
shoots away, retracting
its ovipositor-like tube,
the lid has to go back on
                        quickly.
This material – un-
stable as Ruth's mind
with a half-life twice as long –

needs to be
contained, or it will
smoke on out of here.

❖

The mind in freewheel, clicks
a little cog: catch it.

❖

Carlyle is gathering clues – silky
by entangled
                fistful: emissions, &
clippings – wedges,
flecks unremarkable.

He hoards armfuls & loads them into

the box (hidden
beneath the boards
beneath the bed
in the upper room)

where the sheer
                    diaphanous blows
unceasingly.

(Soon enough, Carlyle says –
evidence accrued will suffice.)

❖

Carlyle wants to know
                    the Why & Wherefore, the lay, suspects:
                                        Nevermore.

❖

Inside the black box, static-y
                    (apocryphal) – this time
what he wants
                    is after-
image, glow – an anchor
for up/down, focus, a light
to balance on, counter
                    song.

❖ ❖ ❖

He's got his bull-dick
                    hat cocked
on, & sleeps by the brim
                    with one eye, open.

❖

more bones, fresh tracks.

                        Carlyle in the morning
warning – weightless –
                    walks across
stone-skin marveling – gaze,
                            gathered
phrase, sluice
            & spillway –
                        falls back into.

                    & then
Carlyle comes up from
                    under – sprawls
upon rocky fragmented – sleeps in the marginal.

❖

carrying various –
                    a rose
into the long waiting
                            .

❖

(with his sleuth-hat on, & a flashlight, just in case)

how – Carlyle asks – how
            do I get out of THIS
        jam? where's the fix?

❖

It's the bony
            vowels he's looking for, sly
divergences, distractions.
                    It doesn't matter
that it's not
            (a probe, a little
embolism, heading for his brain –).

❖

It's the color
        Carlyle's hoping to catch:
fractionary, fragmentary,
& that sharpened line: exquisite
                    excess –
in the night & decompose

            nearby/distant

❖

& that sweet, incessant
                lingering.
You don't want
            to/can't
                shake it loose.
                Like that.

(o

❖

Come this way – he nods –
grabbing a lever, squeezing clutch-stop.

❖

                perfunctorily.
                    Then
Carlyle assists adjust –

it's an old matter.

❖

(& now he can see
  eyebud, the tender

green of bruised
twig-lace, weep –

wall of mangled gape –
                                faces
appearing, that peer
                        into.)

❖

Light metronomic –

it is like a message
                        in octaves
(that only a crew
of intensely
                trained specialists
– committed, devoted, patriotic –
might decipher
                in time).

❖

– rubs (loves)
                        the shine
& lob-lolly, waggle
                        of deflect.

❖

                        o intensest
red among the slack,
lee-side
            of current

water-slung, sprung
from ice bonnet, slush star –
                                still

❖

Carlyle obsessed
                    wrestles limned light –

Obsessed, Carlyle hums
                          a dry little tune, all the same –

Hunkered, he excludes –
                          when he turnsaround, circles:
extends

(& they come).

Carlyle obsessed, backs himself into –
& stands there, listening
                          (before/after, now).

Carlyle obsessed, wrestles dim
                          nebulous –
his legs white and overstretched

(& his blood like a great archway).

(If there should happen
                          to be a headwound, projection
– then Carlyle has won.)

                    Afterwards, before
he is returned (to us), then
he has to wash his hands

                          again & again.

❖

She was pouring out in-
                    to

wide-mouthed, open-lipped
                              (I could see
her tonsils, waggling in there) –
serious,
            repetitive:
                        strings & strings
                                          of intent
yet – and

(How can anyone sleep!
                          with all this singing –
Carlyle mimics, muses.
                        How can anyone think?!)

❖

Of this perishable world, Carlyle knows
next to nothing: flux & hmm – o.
Of the other he cannot tell but wishes.

❖

                                                      for Mough

as she leans over
                        to call
 1.   to her lover
                        below,
 2.   to the depths.

imagines lace & gown, queen-
ruffle – pearls –
                        imagines
blood-scent –
champagne, a crowd
of glitter, sparkling
natter.
            It's small niggle –
Ruth demurs – this hankering
                  & then she turns
                  & walks out into

                    (the snow
& whirling, the darkness, where among
the trees, Carlyle awaits).

❖

From outside
                    Carlyle's looking in
watching
                sway-buckle, loose
knee – the dance.
                    The snow
has piled up on his shoulders
until it is beginning to fill his ears

                                        (this time)
                                    next time:

❖

Carlyle lingers over –
                    lapping

flap of skin. If
emphatically he placed
his mouth on
the bubble of its throat

(bulge of vocal
                    quivering –)

(din-in-ear.)

Through his mouth, in his belly:

❖

When Carlyle puts his mouth
                            over
nostril sheath,

then Carlyle knows
his lungs, soon, will fill with fire.
As it is, already
the smoke is hitting
the roof of his mouth.

❖

Carlyle sings it like a train – out
back, nearby, behind

Mangled, truant –

Carlyle sings it like a train that
                              this time
                              won't even

❖

Carlyle sings it
like a burn victim

                         when it's time
to change the dressings
                         when it's time
to spin the bed
              topside down –

(– so that even
              the muse walking through, weeps
until her surgical
              mask is soaked & sags
from her eyesockets
                   because she can
make Carlyle sing)
              (that song)

❖

      agitated
sets to –
      leans against the drop

(& when his eyes
           zoom down there over)
(& then he has to wonder about

all that strange piping, coming
              up from under.)

❖

           after
my altercation with –
that is to say after
(spurred & bidden) after
my sad, fortuitous woo –

❖

     – &
taking the boy of
the pretty, jaded eyes by hand

leads him
      into.

❖

I'm getting rid of nouns –
         Carlyle informs.
(suggests, hesitates – licks)

❖

     fiercely.)

What's wrong with drift? Carlyle asks,
knowing the anchor's still down there
hooked in brain coral.

❖ ❖ ❖

                              Carlyle & the Hanging Man

– hanging by its neck
                    at full suspend – now
THIS
is something to investigate –

Carlyle circles
hands on hips –
                    jaunty –

circles, 7 times.
Then he makes a sound like a train.

❖

Carlyle cups bone
                    in the bowl of his hand –
its heel,
          that cold inflexible –

then he pushes, watching
                    rigid swing,
the figure 8s
            carved in thin air
eye-height.

❖

when he puts his eye to the hole in the Hanging Man's head

(carefully, he doesn't want to

                                start that swinging
again)

       all he sees is gold

❖

                                      (this time)
When Carlyle comes to investigate
he sees the Hanging Man has been exchanged.

❖

(approaching, the woman wore a mask – close
fitting – expressionless – slack – so that

when she saw the Hanging Man for the very first time – no
gesture informed, betrayed – no tic – no o! – only

the movement of pupil – black – in its slot – quick)

❖

                                (now) Carlyle
plays its bones, xylophone
tones – rib-tacular, fan-
tabulous – stacked sound –

                       brain pate
                       mandible
                       tibia/fibia

       quicker now now double
time –
       with a bone, stolen
from another Hanging Man's corpse.

❖

Carlyle sits across, cross-
                 legged –
they are eye-to-eye
       (at last)

(but the Hanging Man's are plucked
& besides, Carlyle never blinks)

❖

sliver-lit by the quarter moon – sings –
until the sky begins devolve – lightens, defines –

& the wind begins to swing – him

❖

no one much pays attention to
the Invisible Man . . . & for that
he is envious of the Hanging Man's swing – snaps
his fingers & bobs his head in time
                                        to it –
& if he hums a long refrain?

❖

The Hanging Man shivers like a skin, turned outside – thin.

❖

                                                              (   )

finds the skin in a pile
shakes it out   (heavy, wet, cold)
tries it on

              but first – & fortunately –

bare-naked, steps in

(he grabs the Hanging Man's skin
by the hips, & drags it up, on, to
                                himself)

& then he backs his fists
into sleeveholes – arms – hunches
                                into –
like a one-piece suit.

It's the face-
mask – head balloon – that troubles
adjust – as it slithers
into place
              alternately

❖

after a night, thick with dreams

(they crowded through his skull
                              like an emergency
              unretrievable)

Carlyle hankers.
It is a flavor
              at the base of his throat
                    where bones meet
                              surround

(where the rope went, or could)

❖

                                        (just in case)
offers arc
of thorn – broken
from white
              embankment: rose & rouge
twist – gnarled –

a half-crown, tiara –
lays it beneath the Hanging Man's feet.

                                        (next time–

❖

from farther, when –

              Carlyle is searching everywhere
              for the Hanging Man –

hullo. hullo.
          − *how*
could he have lost
          such a thing?

❖

The decapitated man holds his head under his arm & walks off.

(He is looking for the Hanging Man, too − to see how it could have been, otherwise.)

❖

− air-spangle − disruption,

❖

coming around −
Carlyle finds where the Hanging Man once was

         perturbation/anomaly

a hole where gravity came through −

❖

you go anywhere −
         come across −

(glade full of sun & spark,
red-whiffle − toss −
         on one knee
gratefully)(speaking)

         & there's that
very same, exact
         horizontal −
the Hanging Man
         hung from.

❖

(with his breast split,
                    rib-halves hanging like wings)

❖

The son of the Hanging Man
lays
      longside.

The white sun – flattens.

                              Sometimes
the wife of the Hanging Man
                          watches over –
from within
the shadow of the grove, squinting – biting
her hand.

❖

The song of the Hanging Man
                              haunts prevail – even
Carlyle remembers

the wife of the Hanging Man
                          on her cot
with the moon blowing in.

❖

When Carlyle puts on his body mask –

from his store of   & disposables,
from the locked box –

silver-blue, like the body of an eel
                              & muscular
then Carlyle knows what it feels like to be contained.
Then he tapes his mouth shut
& slams the visor down –

he wants to hear the one
                              true song.

❖

the wife of the Hanging Man
                              has put on her mask –
& the boy –

they stand back-to-back

❖ ❖ ❖

uncritical, commensurate –
Carlyle toys with deploy –

how he wants to
                    send his eyes out
into the dark, through
                              the open door (that

❖

                    Carlyle transported
traces arc of move:
flagellant, osmotic

variant pulse-light, queer
& stellar

                    dazzle on the 2nd
plane, unnamed.

                              (little
glow-worms, wiggle-strife
                    brightest in the dark)

❖

          I know – I died
best,
          by the temple of the beak,
                              bird one.

❖

                    (Carlyle warns:
do not justify; do not
                    explain.)

❖

My white wings – damp
                    & under, where
light rarely lingers

          lifted   (up into)

refine

                                        (trembling)

          above
the rack

(& looking down) –

                    after

❖

Carlyle suggests: leap
                    towards – ?

(twig,
     bones – the rose-
stump, thorn-stalk
               rouge-in-drift . . .

& it's cold – settled – crust
like stone
          star-burrs in the heaved-up
                         blow) the moon

❖

since I
        rose, light
& eager —
                never, ever
the lingering

& every other:
                myth-fictive

& then the day
like a tezerat —

always the slow
dragging forth

chatter-natter
                all those
words

to _____ to _____ .

❖

[   ] form —
                inchoate —
[   ]

❖

& so he knew I had the scar, & reaching
                                        behind
felt of it — raised ridge, burl
                        between —
& ran his hands on down

(it was as if
            the stars & all their enemies had
conspired towards
                some monumental loss)

suggests: a little warmed oil rubbed

$$\text{on it} -$$

❖

When Carlyle turns

        his back, it's an amazement
        (& I don't mean maybe).

All you'd want

        to do, is stroke stroke stroke –

contour & flex –
relief & ribbon-

        text.

It is like a map

        to everywhere (allatonce)
        permanent, indwelling.

❖

        epileptic-
           like,
flails flash & spasm –

        under, before
the last; &

❖

              mercilessly.
It can

      move along under   (& does)
           at whim –

flaps through

      (arm belly heart) – bone blade.
                        Also,

tic & shiver

      that settles, surrounds

$$(\text{eye} - \text{I}).$$

❖

When Carlyle stands on
                    bottomlessness
(slough-puppy is down there, in it, lapping
at the soles of Carlyle's bare feet: stark-

                                        ravening)
because of the sound
                    coming up-from
                                        under
(pizzazz & blaring)
Carlyle has never

                              (in his left
                                        hand, squirming)

(then) (& therefore)

❖

As soon as I spoke (it)
                    it went from my head.

(intimation)
                    vowel, mouthful (of)

Better to scatter –

give them all away
                    (one by each)(like roses) – who
needs to know the way?

Carlyle hisses: (reward)
now you're at it, boy.

❖

          bleached –

          splendor-arc, &
the attachment
                    of it

         (I thought I
                    knew that
arc & plummet
                    from somewhere;
I thought I
          recognized
spine-thrust,
               jolt.

I thought he was dead.
Now look.)

❖

All he wants to do
                    is weep weep weep –
poor little
               this one, old little little
                              (dead)

❖

Invisible, Carlyle invites
                    suspend –
When Carlyle succors
                    lay,
he thinks of splendor:
                    arc & curve

                    & the moist
under-lure (the passing
of one thing
               into

❖

what piques fancy, hones
the brain-thorn,
brittle harp – lyre –
                    inflames

❖

The beautiful room is empty.   (for now)

Carlyle has moved on
                    out towards –
                    Still
I can hear the bell-
                    song, &
his intertwining.

❖

& then one day
                (despite
contrary)

Carlyle observes the moon, coming up-down
                                        outside of
its usual.
            That's the place then, that
far notch he marks & notes

(slywise, with his eyes askew & glancing
                                        orb-light: pale
as he jots
        ephemeral
        inferences into
                        the book.

And then he slams it shut, like that.)

(And then he laughs, heartily,
with his head thrown back, far –
& his skin is so thin &
                        white
you can see that
                ridged tube
        & the air
going in & out & its warbling)

❖

I just slept around it –
said Carlyle of the snoring

(& of the real &
)

❖

(& that's when he takes that old
                            albatross

– string-arc & curve –

& swings it

& the sound of it
                  up there
in the air, just above
                  – *whussz, whussz* –
                                      circling
is deeper-drone,
            under.

❖

then, having chosen, Carlyle closes
                            old wounds
with his fingertips –

❖

pallor-stricken
            diffuse – you
can see clear through
– eglantine –
twig, the entire
marsh, beyond –

& the moving
            globes of light,

❖

Carlyle says of/to
                his ghost:
                You Old
thing you. &

takes it by its hand.
Come along, that's enough of that
                                now –
& puts his finger in its mouth
& rubs its gums.

❖

during immerse – elongation –

his breath passes over –
                        narrowly –

                intermingles.

❖

I am still & dead.
When a child pokes Carlyle with a hollow reed
                                he doesn't flinch
                (he is like luxurious
                        a bulwark against)
& when his stone-ness comes up through
                                the staff

perturbation, anomaly
                in the struck-fold, field

then he is immersed in the light that comes up over
& falls like a veil
                across.

❖

even asleep he dreams of sleep.
awake: he dreams

        (already the dread)

❖ ❖ ❖

                           Carlyle Trepanning

                               (this time)
the disc that Carlyle palms
                comes from his (own)
skull – wafer
of moon – lozenge –
which he places on his tongue,
                    swallows –
& it grows & grows.

❖

When Carlyle bores a hole
                in his skull
it's a way to let the Gods in
                (out) –
cylinder, chute

❖

Carlyle sings:

        If you get to heaven   (repeat)
               Before I do   (repeat)
       Just bore a hole   (repeat)
            And pull me through!   (repeat)

                     (& now repeat
                the whole w/o repeats)
sings both parts, lustily.

❖

I *ainagonna* GRIEVE my Lord no more!

❖

The next thing Carlyle knows
he's drilled a hole – (o,
                            Beloved)

in the skull of the boy

& sucks out a sphere – this
he gives back
                    to –

❖

                              :high,
                                unmanageable –
wind –
            surfeit & invite
                        tunnels/pummels

Carlyle's braincase.

It's like startle in there.

❖

a way
        out, into
golden molded light
        sculpted
                    gloss

❖

& now the tears gutter
                        eye-crook to earhole
– remote – lying on his back

(while all around
                they step into
– magnify, manifest –
                        & put their muzzles
                                        up over
brow-shank – drink).

❖

not like dreams
                but just before

❖

                – perilous –

star-river arcing, tracing
sprung rib –
                the moon
molten in the small of his back
like a pool

& when he breathes he breathes in time with it
                                        rhyming
the orifice

❖

& so he turns it
                over –
o he knows his eyes are turning
                                        (milky)

                        upwards
                        towards

THE IOWA POETRY PRIZE and
EDWIN FORD PIPER POETRY AWARD
WINNERS

1987
Elton Glaser, *Tropical Depressions*
Michael Pettit, *Cardinal Points*

1988
Bill Knott, *Outremer*
Mary Ruefle, *The Adamant*

1989
Conrad Hilberry, *Sorting the Smoke*
Terese Svoboda, *Laughing Africa*

1990
Philip Dacey, *Night Shift at the Crucifix Factory*
Lynda Hull, *Star Ledger*

1991
Greg Pape, *Sunflower Facing the Sun*
Walter Pavlich, *Running near the End of the World*

1992
Lola Haskins, *Hunger*
Katherine Soniat, *A Shared Life*

1993
Tom Andrews, *The Hemophiliac's Motorcycle*
Michael Heffernan, *Love's Answer*
John Wood, *In Primary Light*

1994
James McKean, *Tree of Heaven*
Bin Ramke, *Massacre of the Innocents*
Ed Roberson, *Voices Cast Out to Talk Us In*

1995
Ralph Burns, *Swamp Candles*
Maureen Seaton, *Furious Cooking*

1996
Pamela Alexander, *Inland*
Gary Gildner, *The Bunker in the Parsley Fields*
John Wood, *The Gates of the Elect Kingdom*

1997
Brendan Galvin, *Hotel Malabar*
Leslie Ullman, *Slow Work through Sand*

1998
Kathleen Peirce, *The Oval Hour*
Bin Ramke, *Wake*
Cole Swensen, *Try*

1999
Larissa Szporluk, *Isolato*
Liz Waldner, *A Point Is That Which Has No Part*

2000
Mary Leader, *The Penultimate Suitor*

2001
Joanna Goodman, *Trace of One*
Karen Volkman, *Spar*

2002
Lesle Lewis, *Small Boat*
Peter Jay Shippy, *Thieves' Latin*

2003
Michele Glazer, *Aggregate of Disturbances*
Dainis Hazners, *(some of) The Adventures of Carlyle, My Imaginary Friend*